I0504583

YOUR LIFE!

Overcoming Setbacks in Your Life.

Pat-Mae Efe Ezidiegwu

Copyright © 2021 Pat-Mae Efe Ovuworie Ezidiegwu
Favor International LLC
All rights reserved.
ISBN: 9798612601999

DEDICATION

This book is dedicated to everyone who will discover themselves, discover their unique talent to solve problems for the benefit of the human race.

TABLE OF CONTENTS

ACKNOWLEDGMENTS

A big thank to family, relatives and friends, Jaycee, Ephraim, Daniel, Mary, Cyril, Regina, Bridget, Angela, Anne, Patrick, David, Eunice, Fidelis, Helen, Esther, Julie, Felicia, Grace, Evelyn, Tony, Bibian, Steven, Stella, Daniel, Theresa, Christian, Keith, Rachel, Ryan, Mandi, Met, Mrs. Olugbade

FORWARD

I have an urgency to get this book to you as soon as possible and I encourage you to pass it on to your loved ones and everyone. This book is available in Spanish, French, Russian, Vietnamese, German, Filipino, Italian, Japanese, Arabic, Chinese, Hindi and Nepal for global reach. I am so happy to share this book when most people wanted to do the same but death snatched them away to another world. This book is about your life. The reason most people are depressed is because they do not know who they are, they do not know their talent. This book will help you discover who you are, the unique talent to solve problems for the benefit of the human race. When you recognize who you are and you are working towards your life purpose, your life has an exciting meaning. Life is like a quadrant, a quadrant is an instrument for measuring altitudes of a graduated arc of 90 degrees with an index and a plumb line, to show vertical and horizontal direction. Like a Quadrant, this book serves as an instrument for moving you to the life path you want the right way with the tools to change your life in the direction of your dreams. This book was developed through- out my life as far as I can remember from the age of nine; however I did not decide to write this book until my brother-in-law died on July 9, 2017 and did not resurrect from death. Please see my sister's story in chapter 2 of this book, supernatural living, there is a supernatural power available for you to overcome hardship that was meant to stop you, this supernatural power fuels you to do greater exploits. Chapter 1 is about discovering yourself, I share stories of how I found myself and my purpose. Chapter 3 is about Life of possibilities. Jonathan was in coma and his out of this world restoration story will amaze you, life is not over until you say it is over. Chapter 4 is a heart-warming story of the need for true con- nection with the right people, because when you face the triple trouble of life, you will need a person or two to hold you up from losing it. Chapter 5 is the difference confidence makes in life, what are you thinking about yourself? What are you saying to yourself?

INTRODUCTION

In your journey of life, you must have a plan to achieve your purpose. There must be time to think, decision time, working time, unstoppable time and celebration time. You are full of Divine gifts and ability, you must resurrect. This book is to let you know you have the power to resurrect those gifts and ability, you are unstoppable. Life is a battle filled with many setbacks and triumphs, setbacks are stepping stones to triumphs. Your life is for something great. I hope that you will never be stopped again, it is alright to take time to rest. When the road is rough, 1. Resolve all relationship strain by forgiving yourself, forgiving those who offended you, rest the mind and body 2.Spend time with family members, spend time with friends/strangers; 3.Talk to God in His word; 4.Take a walk in nature and seek new ideas, learn something new 5. Know your ability and that you are unstoppable 6. Think on words and moments that confirms the unstoppable in you and paste on board daily; 7. Read your goal board daily; 8.Use-positive self- talk and positive imagery daily; 9. Listen to cheer songs or write your cheer song as simple as: "Thank you...., Thank you..., Thank you... times 3." 10. Dance/exercise and call yourself: Great!

:). Rest resets your core that may be tired from life battles. Be refreshed, you are unstoppable, you are out of this world! Yes! Yes! Take back your exuberant and enthusiastic life now and live it with gladness. You are like a pebble in the ocean of life, exuberant and enthusiastic life lifts up everyone around you. No matter how small or big the setbacks are, they are really a step up for a triumphant life.

CHAPTER 1
DISCOVERING YOURSELF

The picture of Niagara Falls, New York which I visited in June 2015 immersed in me a powerful imagery of power, majesty and unstoppability that you and I share. It depicts how you and I as pebble have huge and lasting ripple effect. Please close your eyes for sixty seconds and imagine the freedom, beauty, power and awesomeness of the waterfall, you are greater than the waterfall in all its freedom, beauty, power and awesomeness. Some years ago, I was able to share this awesomeness to with a person who was in the hospital for multiple suicidal attempts. In this life moment we both shared is unforgettable, indescribable and invigorating! You look beyond yourself daily to be there intentionally for the other person and feel the freedom, beauty, power and awesomeness like Niagara Falls experience.

You can recover from that setback. I want you to know that you do not have to settle for the life you do not want. You have the freedom to use time for what matters to you the most. You can live your dreams and touch the global community. This book is written to inspire you to know who you are and use your power. Take a moment now to 1. Write seven sentences describing who you believe you are. 2. Write seven life passion that makes you happy. 3. Write seven negative life situation that stops you from being free to live your dreams. 4. Write seven ways you need to forgive yourself for contributing to some of the negative life situation. 5. Write seven names of persons you need to forgive for contributing to some of the negative life situation. 6. Write seven things that you fear the most. 7. Write seven actions you need to take in six months now that you have forgiven all including yourself and have no more fear, but faith.

Life trials or what I call battles have transformed me to live exuberantly. What kept me from losing it when I went through the battles of life? I believe it is intimacy with God by Jesus Christ's sacrifice and the sweet fellowship of the Holy Spirit and the quality people he put in my life to rescue me. I still experience life battles but it no longer has power over me. I have walked through the valley of the shadow of death four times and each time the Lord's miraculous delivering power and quality people rescued me so I can tell my story to the world.

I found myself as early as nine years old, that unstoppable me. I knew who I was and I knew that I was going to be a pioneer in many ways. I walked with God confidence that I can do whatever I set my hands to do. I had no concept of impossibility, with God all things are possible. It became clear to me at the age of 13 that I am going to be an attorney and I began to pursue this purpose, thanks to my God-sent teacher, Mrs. Olugbade at Ideal Girls High School, Randle Avenue , Surulere, Lagos, Nigeria who helped me discover who I am and believed in me.

Patti Bom Bom as I was popularly called is a name that always lifted me up; makes me feel like an invisible and incorruptible princess during my childhood. I grew up with a great sense of free-dom and immutability. As early as I can remember, I have wanted to be the best... I wanted to be the greatest. At about 9 years old; I started out asking people who I believe knew better: "what are the two best profession in the world? I was told: doctors and lawyers; hum..mm...mm. I am so thankful to God that he inspired me to attend college when I did and that He made me strong to pursue my life dream of becoming an Attorney and setting up a law office in the year 2000 when it seemed impossible.

Some people were more excited for me than I am for finding my life purpose. Some others discouraged me because they felt that being a lawyer is dangerous, they told stories of how the lawyers they know were harmed in the course of their profession. Others said that law is academically challenging and wondered if I can pass the exams involved. Others stated that, I can always get married to a lawyer instead of being one myself.

But this discouragement did not stop me. I was determined to take action. I am going to go ahead and do what I know I can do. Thank God for who God is in my life, at the age of nine I believed with my whole heart that God created me to be the head and not the tail and that all things that are impossible are now possible because I believe in Him. I applied to sit for the Joint Admissions and Matriculations Board Exam, (JAMB), a Nigerian entrance examination board for tertiary-level institutions. The board conducts entrance examinations for prospective undergraduates into Nigerian universities. The first time, I passed, but I was not admitted to the university to study law because of what is called the Quota system in Nigeria. I applied again for the second time and I was told the same quota system is an obstacle. Someone in Bendel state university Abraka offered that I apply to the Bendel state university to study any course, the game plan was for me to take the JAMB exam while in the first year in the university and then I will be admitted easily for law since I am in the university. For the third time, I took the JAMB exam to study law while I was in Bendel state university and applied to River State University to study law. I made a vow to God that if He makes the impossible become possible, I will serve Him all my life. To my great surprise, God made it possible, I was admitted to study law at the River state university. I travelled to the Rivers State University from the Bendel state university. I visited the university to find my name on the admission list and was so overjoyed that God would favor me this way after much waiting. God is a true God. He is a God who speaks and makes it come to pass when I believe and take appropriate action according to His words.

I went to live with one of my special sisters and her husband in the same city as my new university. The next morning I was preparing to go to class, as I picked up the phone to make a call, I collapsed. I was rushed miraculously to the hospital where I was told I had typhoid fever. I have been blessed up to that moment that I did not understand what it meant to be sick. Ignorantly and innocently, I flushed all the medication the Physician gave to me down the toilet because the smell of the medication made me feel like throwing up. By the time I recovered and went to the university to begin the study of law, it was mid-semester, and I missed most of the introductory lectures.

A major lesson I learned from this set back is that I cannot die (leave this world in the body) until I have accomplished all that God and I have discussed about accomplishing in this world. I truly believe that without a reason to live I would have been dead from the typhoid fever attack.

Ezi at the Supreme Court of Nigeria Abuja

The Comet

TO LIVE IN TRUTH IS TO SERVE

NO. 365   MONDAY, JULY 3, 2000   http://www.cometnews.com.ng

Na'Abba moves to Kano to save his seat
Politics ... Page 15

Owena Bank dons new name today
Executive Jobs ... Page 26

NFA and Coa Bonfrere's N9 pay
Sports

No room for independent candidate in new electoral law

From Wahab Gbadamosi, Abuja

CAMELITE & FAVOUR PAINTS

•Continued on Page 2

Bank rates crash as govt injects N90

• Rates down to three-year

By Olafunde Kazeem, Finance Reporter

Manufacturers angry with NSITF

By Gbadebo Kazeem, Senior Reporter

Okadigbo replies Enwe

By Our Rep

OLUWALOGBON MOTORS LIMITE

Offers

Special Discount, Free Ser
From 26th June, 2000
On
ALL PEUGEOT VEHICLES PURCH

Ogunde's granddaughter makes directing debut

By Gbadamola Arinola, Arts Editor

Governors meet in Abuja on minimum wage

Examples of life setbacks:

1. Manny states "I was forced by my parents to be an Engineer and I lost my job as an Engineer after 5 years".
2. "I have been experiencing depression since my son died"
3. 'I smoke a lot of vape to help me cope with depression due to inability to attend college because I have to work to care for my sick mom'

You too can find and live your life purpose by 1. Writing 7 sentences describing who you believe you are and what makes you happy. 2. Write 7 life passions of yours, the first being the one that you are most passionate. 3. Write 7 problems your first passion will solve for humanity in a way that no one else can. 4. Take action to move your passion from dream to reality

Chapter 1 bonus: Access bonus content online by visiting: http://d4wfh.urlit.us

CHAPTER 2

THE LIFE OF THE SUPERNATURAL

O nce upon a time there was a Knight. He was said to be one the most powerful knights there would ever be. His father was wealthy, which meant he would inherit much money. One bright sunny day, he thought to himself "what am I in the world to do? What is my purpose? He has been unhappy for about 3 months; the main reason he felt unhappy is because the life that he carefully planned out did not come to reality. Being stuck in life is like standing on quicksand; the more you try to get out the deeper you sink. When the knight was stuck he tried to manipulate and control situations by his own wisdom, it made him sink deeper. The knight realized that he had a problem and that he needed someone who has been stuck and is now unstuck to walk with him and show him the way. The knight's realization brought him to EziSystems Solution. Whether you feel stuck for a week or for a year does not really mat- ter. You do the best you can with the oil in your house. Once per- ceptions change, things begin to change. EziSystems SolutionTM explores your purpose; helps you to trust God, helps you focus on what makes you happy; helps you discover your favorite things to do; inspires you to do the things you are good at. The Knight part- nered with EziSystems Solution and lived happily ever after.

What do you do when the life you carefully planned out did not come to reality? My sister escaped being stuck by supernatural intervention. She became stronger after the death of her husband when everyone thought that she has reached her breaking point.

Angieco as she is fondly called escaped being stuck in life when her husband died. Angieco, her husband and child visited USA in December 2016 and left for Nigeria in January 2017.I had the pleasure and joy of seeing my sister again after 14 years and meeting the husband and daughter for the first time. On July 5th, 2017 my birthday, I was in church worshipping and thanking God for all His mercies and favor upon my life. I received a call from my sister and late brother- in-law that evening asking me to pray for his healing. Here is her story.

My husband passed away on the 9th of July 2017. It was so devastating for me. We were highly expectant of open doors of God's blessings and so I felt highly disappointed.

I did not want to accept the verdict of death because I had faith in the God I had served all these years. So I started looking into the word of God that talked about Jesus rising from the dead, I went into fasting, prayed fervently reasoning with the LORD to bring back my husband. I sowed seeds of Resurrection over my husband's life, I went into deep worship and praise professing to everyone that came around me that my husband will rise from the dead. I sowed 20 Christian devotionals into the lives of strangers. I delved into testimonies on YouTube of people raised from the dead.

Little did I know that it was God's will that my husband should be in Heaven with Him. The more I spent time on these spiritual exercises the stronger I felt and the more comfort I received from the Holy Spirit. My countenance was bright and people all around me were amazed of how strong and composed I was in spite of my circumstances.

When my husband was laid in the grave, I finally surrendered to the will of the Almighty God. The spirit of God ministered to me that the situation was all for good. Furthermore, I had personal revelations and others from close associates that my husband was with the LORD and will prefer not to return back to earth.

My daughter was very strong as well, though she missed her Dad a lot. She once said that she wants her daddy to be happy in Heaven and looks forward to us getting reunited back to Him at the close of the age.

Surprisingly my husband's aged parents received the news in good fate, they are very strong in their faith in God, glory to God. After the burial, I went back to my base where I had great zeal for evangelism; sharing the word of God wherever I went, distributing tracts and leading souls to Christ. This further helped to bring healing to the hurt I felt in my soul. I was at peace with myself and filled with so much joy that people who came across me and heard what happened were amazed and inspired by my positive attitude.

So it is possible for you to overcome pain, suffering, trauma, loss. Make a decision to overcome and take corresponding actions accordingly.

Do you want to know the life quadrant of the supernatural? Write 7 life's hardship that is preventing your life purpose from realization. Write 7 actions to overcome. When you have implemented all the right actions towards your life purpose and you experience pain, suffering, trauma and loss and you feel like you are losing it, it is time to connect to the supernatural power. The supernatural turns pain, suffering, trauma and unbearable loss into an advantage to realize your life purpose, supernatural support is available for you at EziSystems Solution.

Chapter 2 bonus: Access bonus content online by visiting: http://d4wfh.urlit.us

CHAPTER 3

POSSIBILITIES IN LIFE

The Quadrant of Possibilities is about life's impossibility circumstance and how to convert life's impossibility to possibility. One day I made a call to Les Brown's company and was awestruck by the voice of the person who answered the phone. It was a voice like I never heard before; it is so full of life with invigorating vibration that I wondered to myself "wow, what a voice, he must have everything going well for him". To my amazement, he told me that he uses a wheelchair for ambulation and I found that shocking and unbelievable.

Here is Jonathan's story:

On January 15, 2014, I was driving from Miami, Florida on I-95 approaching the exit to Fort Pierce, when I failed to turn. Going over an embankment, my body was ejected out of the sunroof ripping my ear off, breaking my neck, back, clavicle, ribs, I landed in a ditch to drown. However, by the grace of God, I was pulled out. As I laid in a coma for two months, the doctors froze my body for seventeen days to test robot on me.

While in my coma my dreams were very vivid. In this dream I lived five lifetimes and the very last lifetime I was a multimillionaire flying from China to Florida, with my beautiful Korean wife. Here is Jonathan in coma.

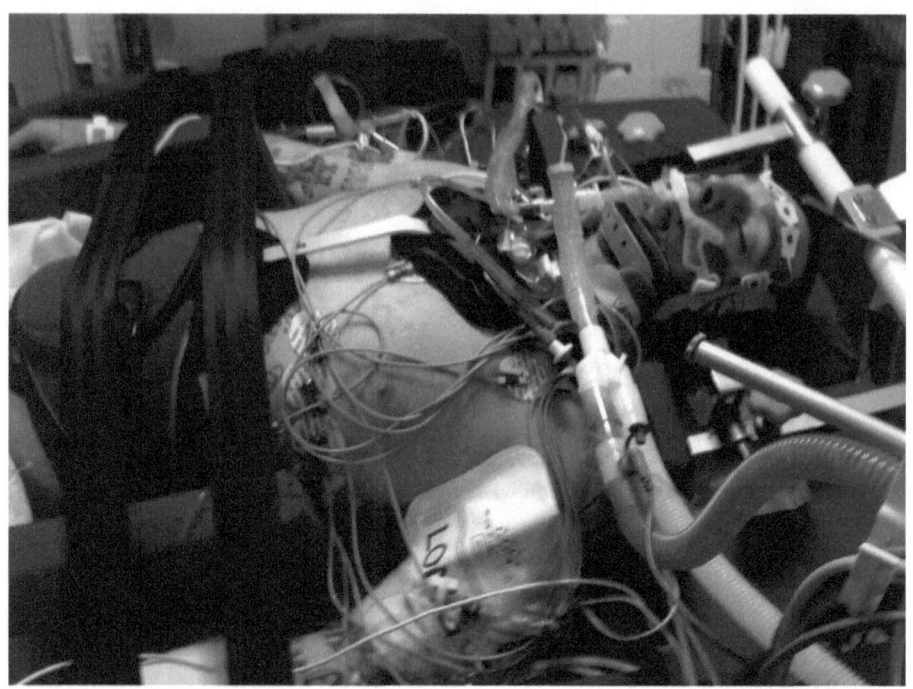

In real life, as a little kid my Grandpa who was called Papa would take me fishing every weekend. My Papa died fifteen years ago, but he appeared to me while in my coma. In one of my dreams, my Papa was the largest fish in the entire world, and everyone wanted to catch him, and I could swim with him. We swam everywhere together and then into his cave where he would turn back into Papa as a man and there was gold everywhere. In another dream, I was up in the clouds with Papa and God looking down at me on the operating table with the tubes in my mouth, tubes in my throat, and tubes in my chest. At that moment I knew the dream during the coma life wasn't real and I hit my knees grabbing God and saying:" Lord, please give me one more chance", tears coming out my eyes, I pleaded: "I won't do the things I've done, I won't be who I was, please give me one more chance." At that very second I awoke from my coma. The doctors told my family on that Friday to go home because I would be dead by Monday. They were also told I would never walk or talk again. When I woke up, I had 24-hour around the clock care, things you do alone I was no longer able to do alone.

I now needed help to get dressed, go to the bathroom, and get to anywhere I wanted to go. The limitations I thought I had and the restrictions the doctors placed on me, held me down for two and a half years.

Eventually, by changing my input, from watching television to reading books, leaving negative people to spending time with people with goals and dreams, from listening to negative music to listen to motivational tapes, my thinking and the course of my life changed.

I now live on my own in Pompano Beach Florida and take care of myself. Going to the Gym every day working out and facing my fears. Today I work for the world's top Motivational Speaker: Les Brown.

I can now do things that I was told I could never do due to the accident. I walked around the gym twice with the help of a walker, and can bench press 235 lbs. By changing my input, I created a fantastic life. At this very moment, at 35 years old, I am a Certified Les Brown Speaker, Coach, and Trainer. My personal business is called, "The Possibilities In You."

This is Jonathan

Chapter 3 bonus: Access bonus content online by visiting: http://d4wfh.urlit.

CHAPTER 4
CONNECTION AND PARTNERSHIP

There is an unseen quadrant of connection and partnership that gives you dominion. For example, as a preteen, teenager, young adult, you may not feel like going to school, going to work or own a business, get married and have kids, it is not surprising to not feel like doing something that you do not understand, all you have to do is to find worthy mentors and ask them the why of life and comply with their advice to prevent stagnation and decay of life. The ruler of a region has dominion over it, and the area itself may be called the ruler's dominion. In the days of the British Empire, Great Britain had dominion over many countries throughout the world.

I met Sun by divine connection at the church, my family and friends conducts monthly outreach to the homeless. On this day, the person who promised to go with us cancelled last minute. I went to church to pray asking God if we should continue with the homeless outreach or cancel. As I opened my eyes, I saw a lady I did not know praying as well and waited to speak with her. When I shared what was on my heart, she gladly came along with me and we experienced open heavens during the outreach.

Sun is a fourth generation Christian from her mother's family, she is living her life purpose as a missionary. In 1997 in New York City (NYC) she was in a state of hunger and thirst for the Lord. This hunger drove her to be baptized by the Holy Spirit and fire.

After that, the Holy Spirit led her to the street to evangelize in NYC every day for three and a half years.

She proclaims the Gospel John 3:16 on street corners in Spanish, English, Chinese and Korean language. She shared the Gospel on Subways and in downtown Manhattan on the weekends before her move to Alaska.

Here is Sun's Story

Three years before 9/11 the Lord placed on my heart the Jabez prayer. Once I began the Holy Spirit informed me that I will be in a new state but I was not told exactly where.

I experienced countless dreams of flying snowy mountain tops, new faces and a foreshadowing of revelations about the end times. I never liked the cold, so I told the Lord I want warmth, a warm place, my heart was set for Florida. One day my mother insisted she wants to move to Alaska. I questioned why she would want to move to somewhere cold and freezing.

But to satisfy her heart I booked a flight and notified the church congregation that she will be leaving for Alaska.

I booked the ticket for mid-august, 2011, a few weeks before her travel time she cancelled the plan for Alaska. She mentioned it would be difficult to move on her own, but shortly after cancelling she insisted on her plan of moving to Alaska once again but this time she was firm.

2-3 weeks later my Husband was laid off from his job, shortly after I was laid off from my job as well. There was a 17 passenger Ford Van parked in front of our square foot city lawn. We decided to fix up the vehicle to embark on a road trip to Alaska.

My mother, father, children, husband and I packed up the van, took off the back seats, placed a bed in the back, a cooler in the car and began our journey to Alaska.

On September 9th, 2011, we reached the Yellowstone Park. The journey to Yellowstone Park took approximately 2-3 days.

While at Yellowstone Park, we abruptly asked about NYC, one man informed us that a building had collapsed; He then explained that the collapsed building is the twin towers. And then I remembered the dream I had about flying white mountain tops

I believe that my family and I would have died in the 9/11 attack in NYC were it not for the unseen quadrant of connection and partnership that gave us dominion to leave New York City 2-3 days before the 9/11 attack.

Upon arriving in Alaska the Lord spoke to me: "Alaska will be the Last Frontier for the nation - worldwide; spiritual and natural reservoir; from now on, I will send you to all nations, Pray - Pray for Alaska"

Do you want to know how to have the quadrant of connection and partnership that gave Sun dominion? What new opportunities do you need to bridge the gap between your life purpose and reality?

Chapter 4 bonus: Access bonus content online by visiting: http://d4wfh.urlit.us

CHAPTER 5

CONFIDENCE IN LIFE

T he quadrant of confidence is an essential mindset for achieve-ment, 80% of life encounters tells you are not up to the task. You have to respond with confidence to all oppositions whether internal or external with the life quadrant of confidence. Fear is paralyzing:

Here is Tiffany's story

Adverse effects of fear and negative thought process:

My name is Tiffany and I would like to tell you my life story in-dicating the importance of our thought process as humans.

I learned through my personal journey of life that what you think about yourself affects your being. Just like a computer, if you put in garbage that is what you get.

Flash back to my elementary and middle school days in West African country Ghana. I was a very smart kiddo. It so happened that in an award ceremony at school at 7th grade, I had a range of 5 recognition as the best student, I was called several times to receive another award before I could even take a seat.

However, in my early days of high school from 9th grade I kind of lost my confidence as an individual. The process was gradual. Its root cause was my thought process. I started believing I was not smart enough and most of my thoughts were negative. These then became the reality as I started seeing it's manifestation in my grades which began to tank.

I heard a rumor in high school that I would have been the prefect/leader, my lack of confidence was permeating into other aspects of my life. The teachers and principal felt I could not handle the job of being a leader when I was in 10th grade so because they did not want me to feel bad I ended up being the library prefect.

It was in 2014 when my mom visited me that she told me my principal in high school asked her what happened to me then, that they noticed I lost my confidence. When I was new to the middle school I was very smart and confident. I remember telling my mom in my last year of high school and my first year of college that I have so much fear in me and I believe I am going to fail my exams.

Here began the long tortuous life of negative thoughts which continues to spiral downwards. The results of continuous negative thought chipped into my confidence and also affected my study life at college. While trying to adjust to life on campus I found out that my college work was so challenging that I was filled with so much fear of failing that I basically could not comprehend what I was reading and I kept having the thoughts in my head that I was a failure.

When it came to the exam, the results of the test arrived and it was exactly as I thought. 'Failure'

A solid support system needed; I was fortunate to have a good support system that uplifted me during those trying times when I had bad thoughts and was losing my self-confidence. My mom is a prayer warrior, we had devotion in the morning before school and at night before beds; we prayed for each other, read the scriptures too.

I remember vividly when I came home from college & I had just failed my exams and I was on my low points, believing I can never be somebody, depression was setting in. I was introduced to a church pastor who counseled me. I learned that depression is one of the most dehumanizing & tiring emotional experiences a person can encounter in their life.

Below is the poem the Pastor gave me to meditate on:

Don't Quit
When things go wrong as they sometimes will,
When the road you're trudging seems all uphill,
When the funds are low and the debts are high
And you want to smile, but you have to sigh,
When care is pressing you down a bit,
Rest if you must, but don't you quit.
Life is queer with its twists and turns,
As every one of us sometimes learns,
And many a failure turns about
When he might have won had he stuck it out;
Don't give up though the pace seems slow--
You may succeed with another blow,
Success is failure turned inside out--
The silver tint of the clouds of doubt,
And you never can tell how close you are,
It may be near when it seems so far;
So stick to the fight when you're hardest hit--
It's when things seem worst that you must not quit.

—Edgar A. Guest

It was a gradual process reversing my negative thought process. It wasn't a smooth ride, but it paid off.

To further instill my new line of thinking, I read the book like 'tough times never last but tough people do' By Robert Schuller. I also joined the campus church, whenever I had a bad time trying to control my thoughts I had my church members encouraging me and praying for me".

Now it's been 18 years since I finally got myself together, and I've been living by this quote from Madeleine L'Engle:

"Maybe you have to know the darkness before you appreciate the light. I have experienced what the dark thoughts do & I never want to go there again".

Count your blessings, even the little ones and be very grateful for who you are. You are unique, there's no one that has the exact same package as you.

You are the apple of God's eye. He will see you through no matter what the journey of life brings you.

Philippians 4:8

Do you want to know how to turn every negative thought that comes through your mind to positive thoughts? Do you want to feel in control and in charge of your life?

Chapter 5 bonus: Access bonus content online by visiting: http://d4wfh.urlit.us

CHAPTER 6
CONCLUSION

L ife is a battle and when you are in the heat of life's battle, everything you know how to do to do not seem to be working, this
because during life battles the fight is to get your spirit, body and
soul to give up the fight. It is tough. Especially when the battle pattern is prolonged with phases of battle arrows coming out to you
one after the other with not even a break, this happened to me.
My spirit almost forgot everything I am sharing with you, after the
arrows of life battle came to me like a machine gun in my body
after 3 separate motor vehicle accident and a plane crash escape.
Be humble to find that quality person who is stoppable from life
battles to lift you up. I met a preteen who told me that she feels
stuck, I have met elementary, middle school, high school and college students who expressed the same feeling of being stuck not
knowing the reason for the feeling. On the other hand, I have also
met rich and poor middle age men and women who told me they
are stuck due to mental health, life problems and disappointments.

I want the whole world to read this book and pass it to their
neighbors, we will give you 10% of the cost of the book as soon as
your neighbor writes to give us your name.

Each day I wake up to the news of someone who is presumed
to be doing excellently well in life commit suicide, I know that that
there other ten unknown persons who committed suicide. I am
shaken to my core and cry out to God to have mercy on humanity
and save us from the onslaught of life problems and disappointments that causes depression. It's time the school system begin to

teach our children the meaning of mental health, life problems and disappointments and positive ways to cope with them.

I know that you now know who you are, that you are the only one on this earth to solve a particular problem for the world. I trust that you also believe in the supernatural assistance for when you have done the best you can in life and your best is not good enough to solve life problems and disappointment. I trust that going forward, you feel emotion but you will allow feelings to affect your behavior positively. I am so excited that you now know that there are abundant possibilities around you and you just need to connect and partner with your destiny helpers with confidence.

I am happy for ever for the NEW YOU who will not let suicide of life, Suicide of dreams take you out from solving world problems.

Please log on to link for consulting to share how you overcame mental health challenges, Life problems and disappointments.

There are also free 30 minutes consulting available on following:

1. Knowing your own stress and Strategies for relieving stress
2. 6 Tips to Keep a Positive Mindset for a Prosperous and Happy Life
3. How to Change Every Thought from Negative to Positive One & Transform Your Life
4. How to Avoid Life's Most Harmful Destructions: bad connection/bad company
5. How to connect to the right connections for life passion/ purpose/path
6. How to Make the Most of the Hand Life Deals You
7. How YOU CAN Transform Your Mindset to Make Your Wildest Dreams a Reality
8. The Secret to Transforming the Impossible into Reality
9. How to Harness Your Unique Talent to Make Top Dollar in 6 Months or Less

10. How to Discover Your Life Path & Take Steps Toward an Ultra-Successful Future
11. How to Overcome Loss & Suffering and Emerge Even Stronger Than Ever Before
12. 10 Positive Affirmations for Getting Out of Your Rut
13. 10 things people can say to YOU to get unstuck EziSystems SolutionTM
14. 10 Powerful Strategies to Get Out of Your Rut EziSystems SolutionTM
15. How to accept your present self but set attainable goals for a better self

ADDITIONAL RESOURCES

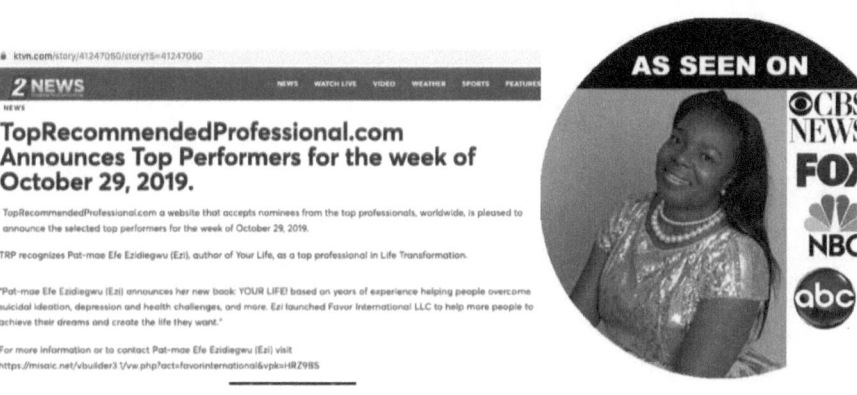

TopRecommendedProfessional.com Announces Top Performers for the week of October 29, 2019.

TopRecommendedProfessional.com a website that accepts nominees from the top professionals, worldwide, is pleased to announce the selected top performers for the week of October 29, 2019.

TRP recognizes Pat-mae Efe Ezidiegwu (Ezi), author of Your Life, as a top professional in Life Transformation.

"Pat-mae Efe Ezidiegwu (Ezi) announces her new book: YOUR LIFE! based on years of experience helping people overcome suicidal ideation, depression and health challenges, and more. Ezi launched Favor International LLC to help more people to achieve their dreams and create the life they want."

For more information or to contact Pat-mae Efe Ezidiegwu (Ezi) visit https://misaic.net/vbuilder31/vw.php?act=favorinternational&vpk=HRZ985

ABOUT THE BOOK

Life is a battle and when you are in the heat of life's battle, everything you know how to do, do not seem to be working, this because during life battles the fight is to get your spirit, body and soul to give up the fight. It is tough. Especially when the battle pattern is prolonged with phases of battle arrows coming out to you one after the other with not even a break, this happened to me. My spirit almost forgot everything I am sharing with you, after the arrows of life battle came to me like a machine gun in my body after 3 separate motor vehicle accident and a plane crash escape. Be humble to find that quality person who is stoppable from life battles to lift you up. I met a preteen who told me that she feels stuck, I have met elementary, middle school, high school and college students who expressed the same feeling of being stuck not knowing the reason for the feeling. On the other hand, I have also met rich and poor middle age men and women who told me they are stuck due to mental health, life problems and disappointments.

ABOUT THE AUTHOR

Pat-Mae Ezi- is a Global EziSystems solution- the founder of Pat-Mae Ezidiegwu chambers, Nigeria, Wealthchase LLC and Favor International LLC. She is an international speaker, Wellness/ Image Partner, Company Partner; Relationships Partner and Author, Trainer and Successful Entrepreneur.

Leveraging her diverse background in the Word, Law, Healthcare, Business, Family and Education, She created EziSystems Solution to transform lives from negative to positive. She is featured on CBS NEWS, FOX, NBC and ABC.

www.ingramcontent.com/pod-product-compliance
Lightning Source LLC
Chambersburg PA
CBHW031505210526
45463CB00003B/1090

* 9 7 9 8 6 1 2 6 0 1 9 9 9 *